THE ARCHISUTRA

May we suggest page 35 ;)

Jessica
+
Scott

THE ARCHISUTRA

The handbook's final chapter

MIGUEL BOLIVAR

TABLE OF CONTENTS

09 PREFACE

11 INTRODUCTION

13 MODULOR MANHOOD

21 GENERAL ARRANGEMENTS

22. LAYING THE FOUNDATIONS
24. TRUSS ME
26. THE PILE DRIVER
28. THE FLYING BUTTRESS
30. EYEBALLING
32. TYPICAL WALL UP
34. THERE'S NO I IN BEAM
36. HARD FURNISHINGS
38. THE REVERSE PILE
40. THE VITRUVIAN

42. THE MAXIMUM RISER
44. THE PLATFORM LIFT
46. BACK TO THE DRAWING BOARD
48. ON PILOTI
50. RANCH-STYLE
52. THE SEATED CONNECTION
54. WHEN IN BARCELONA
56. INTERNATIONAL STYLE
58. THE CHAISER
60. THE SCAFFOLD

62. FALLINGWATER
64. THE HIGH END
66. THE DOMESTIC
68. THE IKEA SALE
70. THE POMPIDOU
72. THE PETRONAS
74. THE BRUTALIST
76. HUMAN FORMWORK
78. THE BOTTOMAN
80. THE BACK SEAT DESIGNER

82. THE CLASSICAL
84. THE NEO CLASSICAL
86. THE CANTILEVER
88. EXTERNAL WORKS
90. OSCAR'S
92. GET AN EIFFEL
94. EAMES IT IN
96. THE VERY GEHRY
98. THE REAL FLEMISH BOND
100. THE POSTMODERN

102. PRAIRIE STYLE
104. THE LAP JOINT
106. IN VITRA VERITAS
108. THE GAUDI
110. ROHE THE BOAT
112. THE ENGINEER
114. THE ALL NIGHTER
116. YOU-VALUE
118. THE TRELLICK
120. THE GOLDEN RATIO

NOTICE

PREFACE

Swiss architect Le Corbusier coined the phrase 'machines for living', within his book, 'Towards an Architecture' in 1923. Sex plays a large role in society and everyday life. So, why is it so often overlooked when an architect designs a building?

The Archisutra raises the question: How should we design for sex?

In 1490 Leonardo da Vinci sketched the Vitruvian Man, a diagram showing the proportions of man based on the writings of Vitruvius in 400AD. The sketch of the Vitruvian Man depicts the perfect male form as seen by Vitruvius. Vitruvius aimed to discover the mathematical proportions of the human body and use the findings to improve the function and appearance of architecture.

In more modern times, the architect Le Corbusier devised an anthropometric scale of proportions, a further development from Vitruvius' work. He called his system The Modulor. The Modulor, was a standard model of the human form used by Le Corbusier to determine the correct amount of living space needed for residents in his buildings.

The Archisutra follows on from the work of Vitruvius, da Vinci and Le Corbusier and pushes the idea that buildings should be designed around human life.

INTRODUCTION

The Archisutra gives anyone the chance to redesign their sex life. The book contains the necessary information about the human body with a selection of sexual positions ready to be put into practice.

The detailed design information and annotated scale drawings within the book, make it easier for you to design spaces or help you convert an existing space.

MODULOR MANHOOD

Taking the name from Corbusier's Modulor, a way of designing using the proportions of man, this chapter gives you the necessary dimensions of the human body and provides some dimensional context moving forward.

Male Scale

Average male body measurements:

The average male body is 1750mm or 5' - 9" tall

Average shoulder height is 1460mm or 4' - 9"

Average chest height is 1315mm or 4' - 4"

Average groin height is 865mm or 2' - 10"

Average hand height is 780mm or 2' - 7"

Average knee height is 515mm or 1' - 8"

Average shoulder width is 355mm or 1' - 2"

355 mm
1'-2"

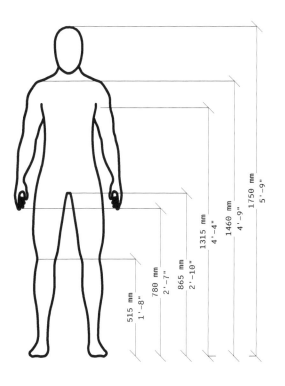

515 mm
1'-8"

780 mm
2'-7"

865 mm
2'-10"

1315 mm
4'-4"

1460 mm
4'-9"

1750 mm
5'-9"

15

Female Scale

Average female body measurements:

The average female body is 1610mm or 5' - 3" tall
Average shoulder height is 1340mm or 4' - 5"
Average chest height is 1205mm or 3' - 11"
Average groin height is 820mm or 2' - 8"
Average hand height is 730mm or 2' - 5"
Average knee height is 465mm or 1' - 6"
Average shoulder width is 310mm or 1' - 0"

310 mm
1'-0"

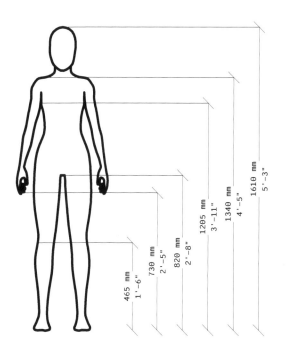

465 mm
1'-6"

730 mm
2'-5"

820 mm
2'-8"

1205 mm
3'-11"

1340 mm
4'-5"

1610 mm
5'-3"

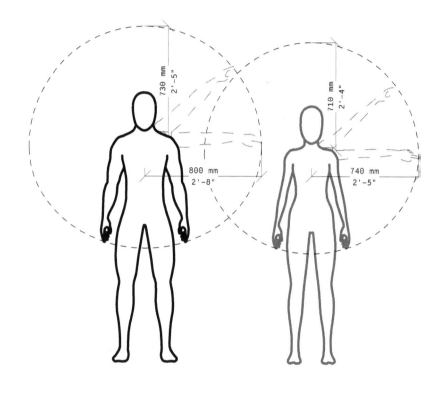

730 mm
2'-5"

800 mm
2'-8"

710 mm
2'-4"

740 mm
2'-5"

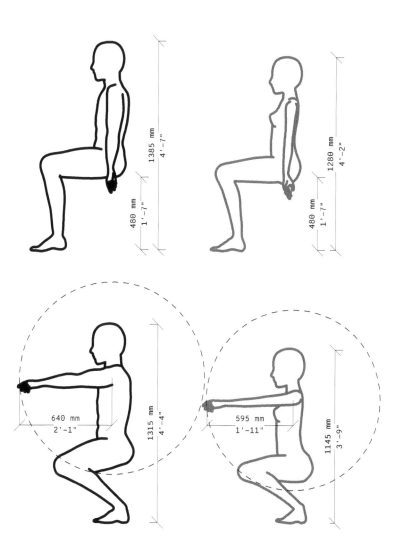

1385 mm
4'-7"

480 mm
1'-7"

1280 mm
4'-2"

480 mm
1'-7"

640 mm
2'-1"

1315 mm
4'-4"

595 mm
1'-11"

1145 mm
3'-9"

GENERAL ARRANGEMENTS

LAYING THE FOUNDATIONS

Typical Location: Mixed Use
Sustainability: High

The first arrangement will give you a good introduction to *The Archisutra* and the mastery of this position will help you with the more complex positions later in the book.

To perform this position, she lays down on a flat surface with her knees bent and her lower legs at a 50 degree angle to the floor. A quick way for her to determine the correct angle is to position her feet 450mm or 1'-6'' away from her. He lays on top of her so that they are face to face adjusting the angle between them.

Best Practice: Lifting her legs higher or adding a pillow to her lower body will alter the angle and allow for more up and down movement. This is commonly known as the 'CAT' or coital alignment technique.

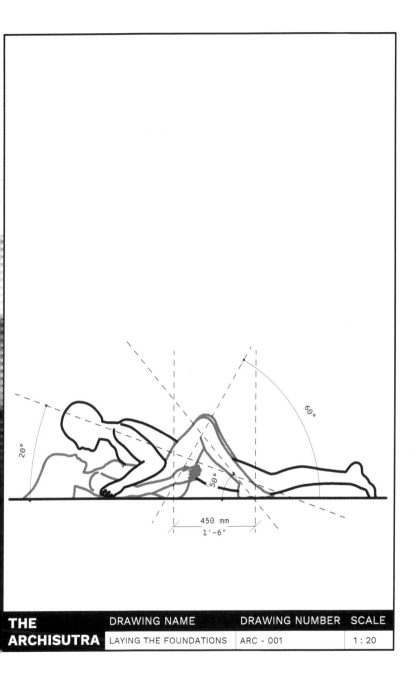

20°

60°

50°

450 mm
1'-6"

TRUSS ME

Typical Location: Mixed Use
Sustainability: Medium

Based on the 'Warren Truss' patented in 1848, this position uses a diagonal arrangement working with both tension and compression. The load acting on the elements is focused towards the centre. In this position he acts as the bottom chord tying the truss together.

The angles within this position are key to its success. It is normally performed on a firm, flat surface with some bounce for assistance. To begin, he lies flat on the ground while she sits on top of him resting her weight in his lap. Her lower legs should be at 90 degrees to her thighs and as she leans back, one hand should be placed on her knee and one on the floor. Her careful positioning provides a stable platform for rotational movement, for further stability he can take hold of her thighs.

Best Practice: This position relies on her correct angular arrangement, if performed without due care and attention there is a risk of injury.

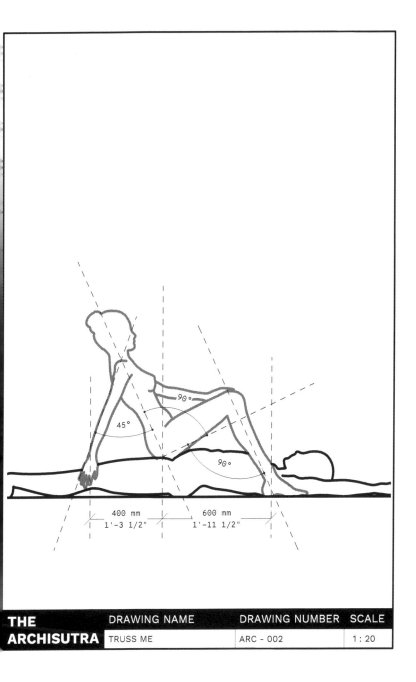

90°

45°

90°

90°

| 400 mm | 600 mm |
| 1'-3 1/2" | 1'-11 1/2" |

THE ARCHISUTRA	DRAWING NAME	DRAWING NUMBER	SCALE
	TRUSS ME	ARC - 002	1 : 20

25

THE PILE DRIVER

Typical Location: Mixed-use
Sustainability: Low

The Pile Driver takes inspiration from the piling machines used to bore deep into the ground to form foundations. Like a piling rig, the force is focused to particular area, however in this case the angle is altered to make the position more achievable.

To begin, he kneels down with the main part of his body perpendicular to the floor. Then, starting in a horizontal position she manoeuvres herself up his body until she is at a 40 degree angle. He can assist by holding her thighs to allow her to get into position.

Best Practice: Using a pillow for support can help to achieve the most effective angle and relieve pressure on the body.

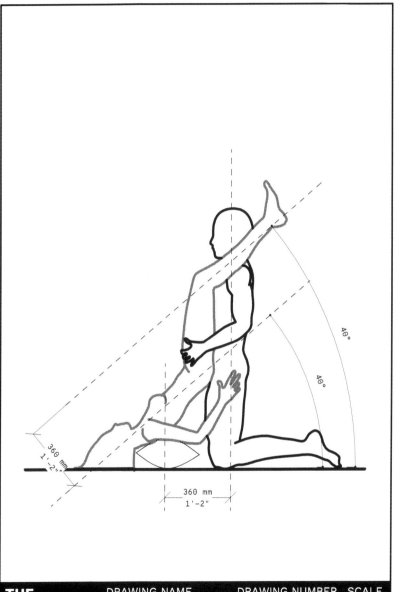

360 mm
1'-2"

360 mm
1'-2"

40°

40°

| THE | DRAWING NAME | DRAWING NUMBER | SCALE |
| **ARCHISUTRA** | THE PILE DRIVER | ARC - 003 | 1 : 20 |

THE FLYING BUTTRESS

Typical Location: Mixed-use
Sustainability: Low

The form of this position resembles buttresses used in medieval architecture, most often associated with gothic churches. The buttress was used to support the vertical building elements and reinforce them against lateral movement.

This position is similar to *The Pile Driver*, but there are a few subtle differences. In this case he acts as the vertical element supported by her body. She wraps her legs around his chest as she pushes and pulls herself towards him.

Best Practice: She should use her arms to pull and push him back and forth.

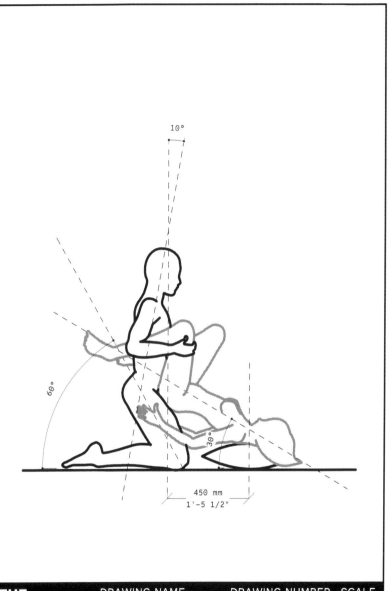

10°

60°

30°

450 mm
1'-5 1/2"

THE	DRAWING NAME	DRAWING NUMBER	SCALE
ARCHISUTRA	THE FLYING BUTTRESS	ARC - 004	1 : 20

29

EYEBALLING

Typical Location: Residential
Sustainability: High

The act of *Eyeballing* something in is done without the use of any measuring device, this position follows a similar method.

To start, both participants stand facing each other about an arms width apart. They then take a step forward with opposite legs and come together into a kneeling position.

Best Practice: Both parties should kneel down in synchronicity and in perfect alignment. This takes time to practice and should be done in complete darkness when mastered fully.

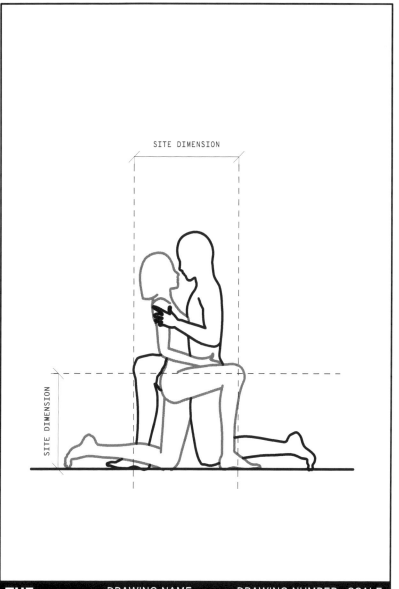

SITE DIMENSION

SITE DIMENSION

THE ARCHISUTRA	DRAWING NAME	DRAWING NUMBER	SCALE
	EYE IT IN	ARC - 005	1 : 20

TYPICAL WALL UP

Typical Location: Mixed-use
Sustainability: Medium

Designed to be practiced on any wall, the *Typical Wall Up* requires strength and dexterity.

Both parties start approximately 285mm or 0'-11" from the wall. Once facing each other, she raises her less dominant leg and he takes hold of it. She then jumps off the ground using her other leg and wraps it around his midriff. He holds the other leg and push her gently on to the wall.

Best Practice: This position is best carried out on a solid external wall to reduce sound transmission.

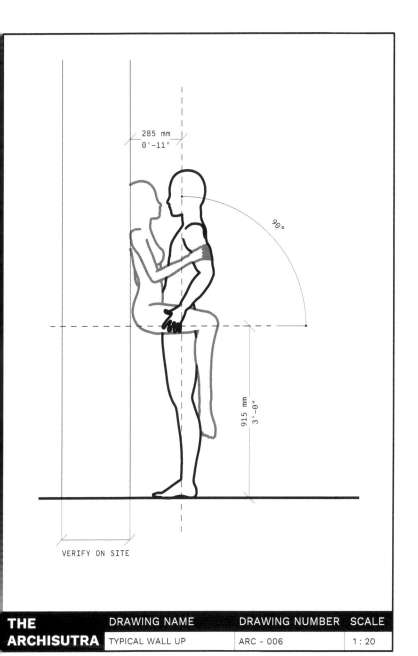

285 mm
0'-11"

90°

915 mm
3'-0"

VERIFY ON SITE

THE ARCHISUTRA	DRAWING NAME	DRAWING NUMBER	SCALE
	TYPICAL WALL UP	ARC - 006	1 : 20

33

THERE'S NO I IN BEAM

Typical Location: Residential
Sustainability: High

This position requires both parties to be synchronized. The position works best when forces are equal and opposing.

To start, he lies flat on the ground and she lies on top of him placing her feet either side of his head. They pull each other closer and then release, repeating the motion and remaining in sync.

Best Practice: It is easier for her to start sitting on his lap before both lean back into the position.

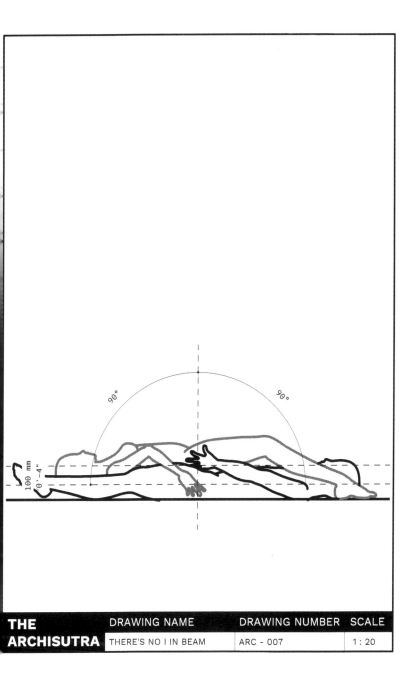

90°　　　　　90°

100 mm
0'-4"

HARD FURNISHINGS

Typical Location: Commercial

Sustainability: High

Using furniture as a platform for sex is nothing new. This position can be performed on dining tables, workbenches, desks etc. Your old furniture could take on a whole new function.

To begin, she sits close to the table top edge leaning back at an angle of 60 degrees. He then pulls her closer as he moves towards her.

Best Practice: The perfect height for this position is dependant on the dimensions of the participants. It is recommended to shop around for correctly sized tables.

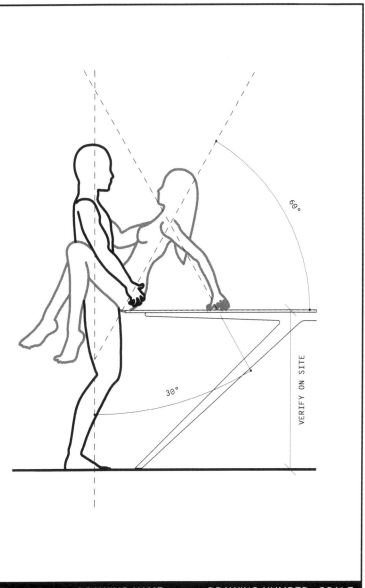

60°

30°

VERIFY ON SITE

THE REVERSE PILE

Typical Location: Residential
Sustainability: High

The Reverse Pile also stems from a piling rig, however this position places her in control from a seated position.

He lies flat and manoeuvres his upper body into a 45 degree angle using his arms as supports. She then lowers herself onto him, using her legs as balancing tools. Up, down and radial movements complete the position.

Best Practice: She should place one foot approximately 200mm or 0'-8" in front of the other to accomplish more complex movements.

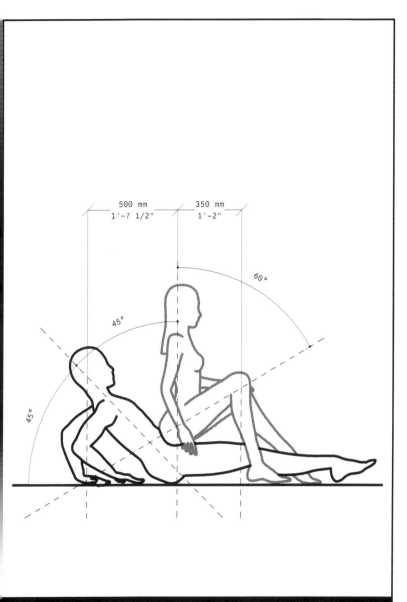

500 mm
1'-7 1/2"

350 mm
1'-2"

60°

45°

45°

THE ARCHISUTRA	DRAWING NAME	DRAWING NUMBER	SCALE
	THE REVERSE PILE	ARC - 009	1 : 20

THE VITRUVIAN

Typical Location: Residential
Sustainability: High

Named after the Vitruvian Man, a drawing by Leonardo da Vinci from around 1490, this position is based on the similarities of ideal human proportions and geometry as described by Vitruvius. Vitruvius believed that the ideal body should be eight heads high and that the human figure could be used to determine the proportions of classical architecture.

To perform this position, she stands upright with her arms outstretched perpendicular to her body. He then stands behind her and widens his stance, lowering his body to the required height.

Best Practice: It is easier when both parties are a similar height, but books, boxes and beds can be used to get a better alignment.

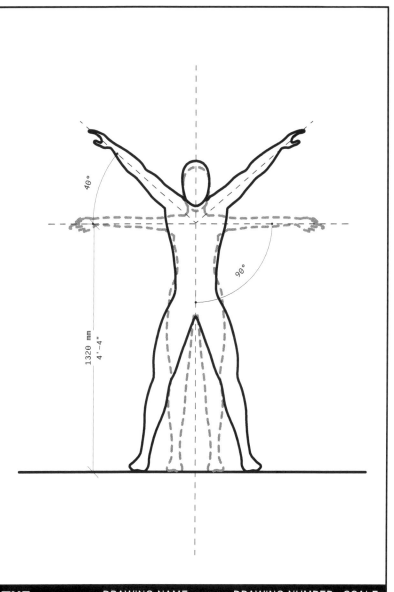

40°

90°

1320 mm
4'-4"

THE MAXIMUM RISER

Typical Location: Mixed-use

Sustainability: Medium

The staircase can be used to conduct a variety of positions. *The Maximum Riser* takes its name from the vertical element in each step.

To perform this position, first find a suitable staircase. To start, she chooses an appropriate step to kneel on - usually the third from the bottom. She then bends forward, resting her hands on the step above, while he stands at the bottom of the staircase and holds her waist at a 35 degree angle to himself.

Best Practice: Remember that building regulations vary between private and public staircases. Public stairs offer the preferred shallower angle.

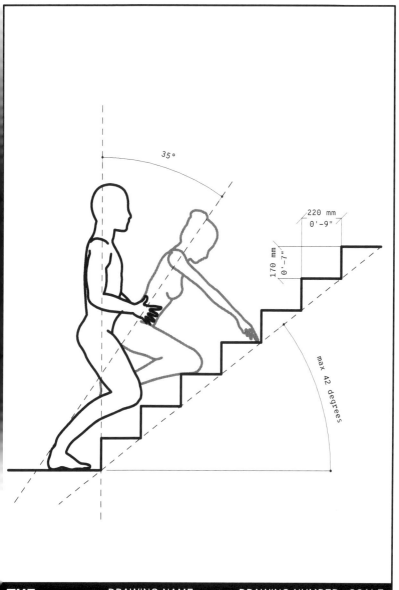

35°

220 mm
0'-9"

170 mm
0'-7"

max 42 degrees

THE PLATFORM LIFT

Typical Location: Mixed-use
Sustainability: Medium

This position bears resemblance to the action of a platform lift used in building construction. It is one of the more advanced positions in *The Archisutra* and should be performed with the utmost care and attention.

The begin, she places a pillow on the ground before laying down with her shoulders resting on it. She adopts the position shown by thrusting her hips into the air, supporting her body initially with her arms. He then moves into position above her, taking hold of her ankles. Once he is in position she lays her arms flat on the ground for stability.

Best Practice: He should support his own body weight throughout to prevent injury.

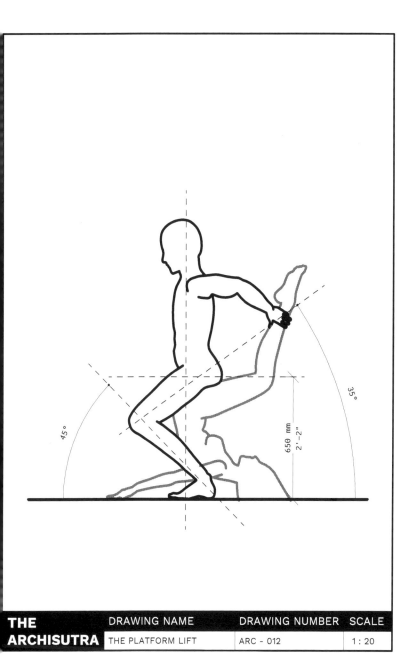

45°

35°

650 mm
2'-2"

BACK TO THE DRAWING BOARD

Typical Location: Commercial

Sustainability: Low

Inspired by the classic but soon to be obsolete drawing board, this position is a test of both strength and balance.

The position begins by first setting the appropriate angle of the table and lowering the seat to a comfortable height. He then adopts the position shown by lying on the table and lowers himself on to the chair. She then positions herself on top of him, holding on to his legs to prevent her falling forward.

Best Practice: For beginners it is recommended to start with the table angled at 10 degrees and move on to a steeper angle once well practiced.

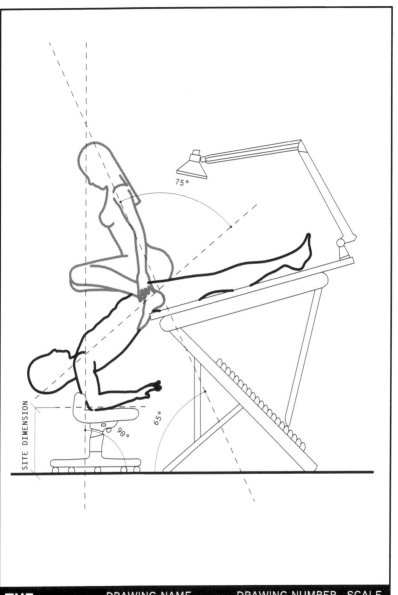

75°

SITE DIMENSION

65°

90°

ON PILOTI

Typical Location: Residential
Sustainability: Low

On Piloti is named after the first of Le Corbusier's five points, which included the use of piloti to raise a building off the ground. Using piloti creates a light and free space beneath a building.

This position requires strength and a strong grip from both participants. Starting in a standing position, he lifts her to the required level. Once in this position she tightly wraps her legs around his waist making the position more comfortable.

Best Practice: Practice in an area with a soft landing.

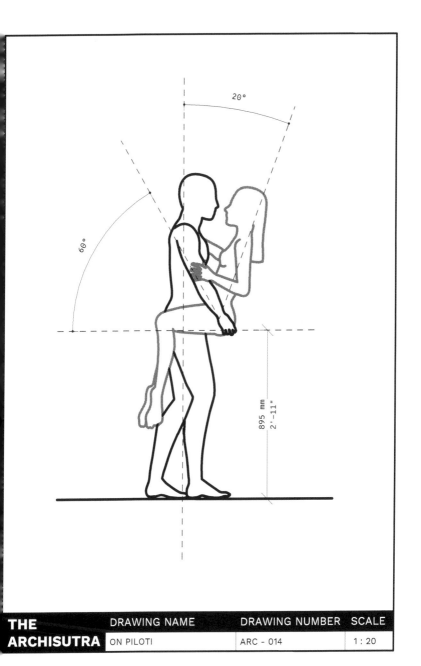

20°

60°

895 mm
2'-11"

THE ARCHISUTRA

DRAWING NAME
ON PILOTI

DRAWING NUMBER
ARC - 014

SCALE
1 : 20

49

RANCH-STYLE

Typical Location: Residential
Sustainability: High

Ranch-style architecture, characterised by a long, low profile and a wide open layout, was popular in middle class post-war America.

To adopt this position, both participants begin by lying opposite each other. She lifts both legs and places them either side of his waist. Pulling each other closer, he grips her below her knees and she holds onto his hips.

Best Practice: He can bring his knees together to tighten his grip.

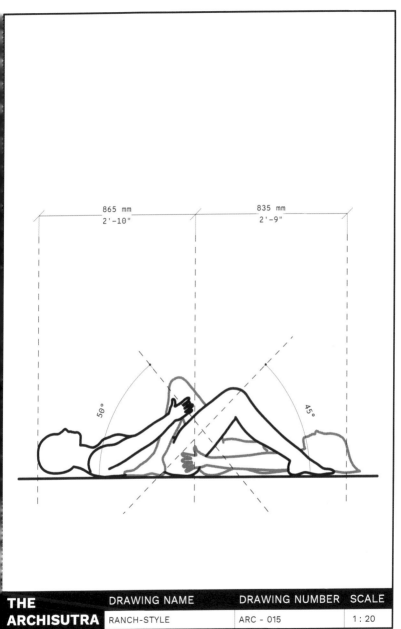

865 mm
2'-10"

835 mm
2'-9"

50°

45°

THE ARCHISUTRA	DRAWING NAME	DRAWING NUMBER	SCALE
	RANCH-STYLE	ARC - 015	1 : 20

THE SEATED CONNECTION

Typical Location: Residential
Sustainability: High

Named after a steel connection with the same name, this position is one of the more intimate positions within *The Archisutra*. The angles of both participants are fixed and the position relies on a pushing and pulling motion.

The Seated Connection is performed as he sits down on a flat surface with his torso at 90 degrees to his legs. She then lowers herself on to his lap, moving her legs around his waist and leaning back at a 30 degree angle. He reaches behind and pulls her closer by holding on to her legs. She maintains a firm grip on his shoulders.

Best Practice: He should not be tempted to wrap his arms around her but instead allow the intensity of the position to increase gradually.

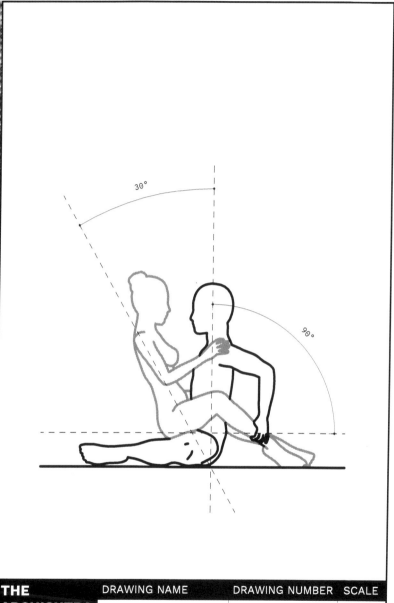

30°

90°

THE	DRAWING NAME	DRAWING NUMBER	SCALE
ARCHISUTRA	THE SEATED CONNECTION	ARC - 016	1 : 20

WHEN IN BARCELONA

Typical Location: Residential
Sustainability: Medium

This positions is inspired by the Barcelona chair, designed by Ludwig Mies van der Rohe in 1929. This famous chair was originally designed for Spanish royalty at the opening ceremony of the International Exposition.

The position begins with both parties facing in same direction at the front of the chair. He stands behind her as she fixes herself in the centre of the seat with her hands clasping the back rest. He takes hold of her hips and with a slightly bent knee, angles her over the edge of the chair.

Best Practice: If you do not own a Barcelona chair, a similar chair or sofa can be used. For best results you should replicate the angles of the original chair.

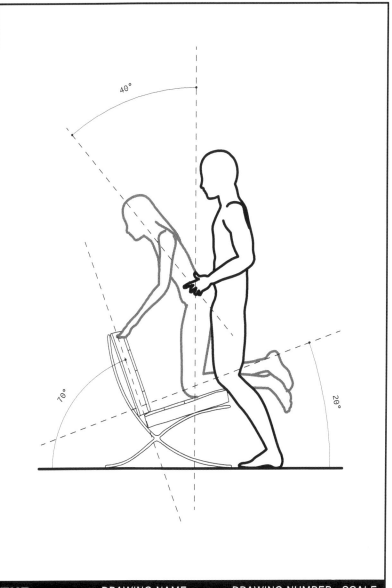

THE	DRAWING NAME	DRAWING NUMBER	SCALE
ARCHISUTRA	WHEN IN BARCELONA	ARC - 017	1 : 20

INTERNATIONAL STYLE

Typical Location: Residential
Sustainability: Medium

The International Style was first defined by American architects Henry-Russell Hitchcock and Philip Johnson in 1932. Focusing on aesthetics, its characteristics include rectilinear forms and surfaces stripped of ornamentation. The style has an emphasis on open interior spaces with a weightless visual quality.

To emulate this style, he lies on his back and lifts his legs forming a right angle with his knees. She intersects him by positioning herself in a deep squat above him, his legs slot between her thighs and her underarm.

Best Practice: It is important to maintain each angle with precision so that she appears weightless in her squat.

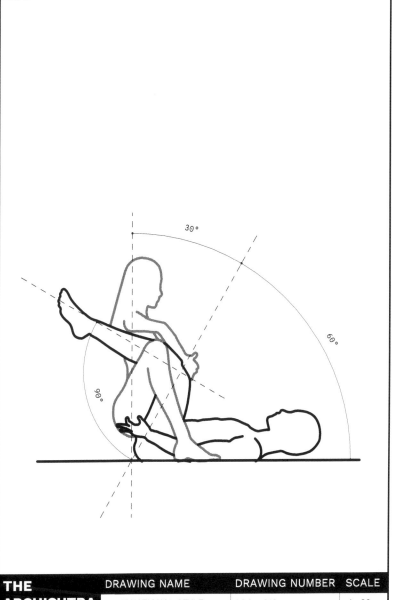

30°

60°

90°

THE
ARCHISUTRA

DRAWING NAME
INTERNATIONAL STYLE

DRAWING NUMBER
ARC - 018

SCALE
1 : 20

THE CHAISER

Typical Location: Residential
Sustainability: Medium

A chaise lounge or sunbed is required for this position, along with a substantial amount of flexibility and strength.

In this position, he creates a platform using the backrest to support his upper body. She then positions herself as shown, leaning on his chest for support. He wraps his arms around her upper legs and at this moment she lifts her legs to form a V shape with her body.

Best Practice: The angle of the back support is key to the success of this position, to avoid unnecessary pressure on both participants.

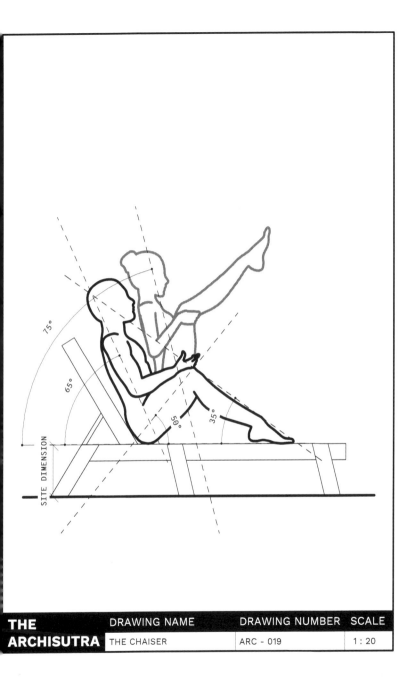

75°

65°

50°

35°

SITE DIMENSION

DRAWING NAME	DRAWING NUMBER	SCALE
THE CHAISER	ARC - 019	1 : 20

THE SCAFFOLD

Typical Location: Residential
Sustainability: Low

Scaffolding is a temporary structure erected to aid the construction process of a building. This position tests his core strength and requires stability.

To perform *The Scaffold*, he assumes a bridge like form as she slots into his lap at a 70 degree angle.

Best Practice: She should squat in the position shown but should be careful not to exert her full weight to avoid injury.

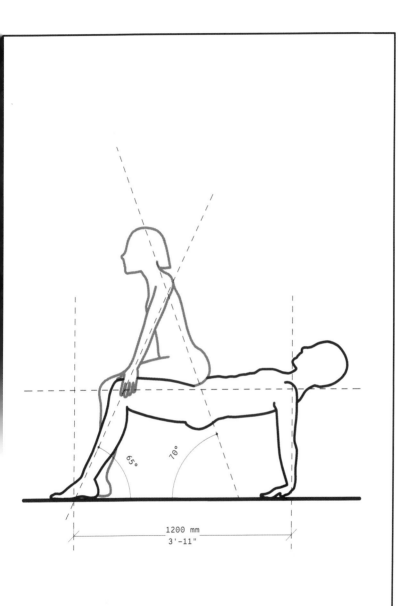

65°

70°

1200 mm
3'-11"

THE ARCHISUTRA	DRAWING NAME	DRAWING NUMBER	SCALE
	THE SCAFFOLD	ARC - 020	1 : 20

61

FALLINGWATER

Typical Location: Residential
Sustainability: Medium

Fallingwater is the name of one of Frank Lloyd Wright's most famous dwellings, completed in 1939 in Southwestern Pennsylvania. Inspired by Japanese architecture, Wright designed the building with an emphasis on creating harmony between man and nature.

He positions himself beneath the flow of water with his legs in front and his back angled at 70 degrees to the ground. She kneels on all fours with her knees and arms positioned at either side of his legs.

Best Practice: If you don't have a waterfall nearby, you can practice in the shower. The water should fall equally between his chest and her back.

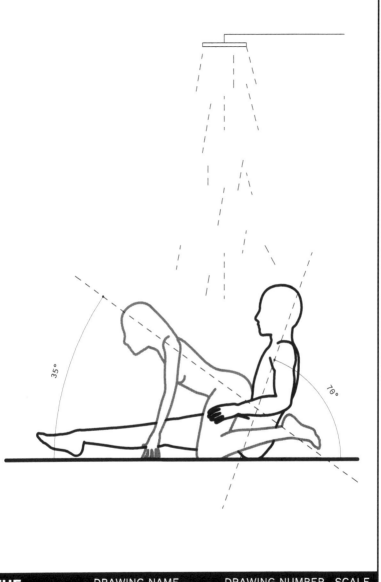

35°

70°

DRAWING NAME	DRAWING NUMBER	SCALE
FALLINGWATER	ARC - 021	1 : 20

THE HIGH END

Typical Location: Residential
Sustainability: High

The classic Eames Lounge Chair was the first chair Charles and Ray Eames designed for a high-end market. Herman Miller highlighted the versatility of the chair which featured in apartments and townhouses designed for the super wealthy.

In this position, he sits fully back in the chair with his feet off the ground. She sits on top with a straight back and her arms stretched to his shoulders.

Best Practice: Add the ottoman to prop up his feet for a first-class experience.

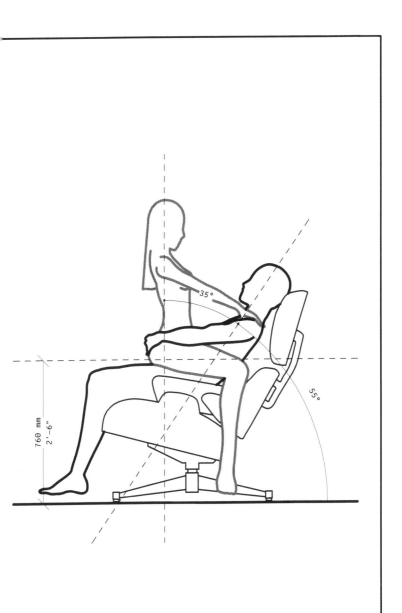

35°

55°

760 mm
2'-6"

THE DOMESTIC

Typical Location: Residential

Sustainability: Medium

Domestic appliances and white goods within the home are often fixed at waist height, providing a perfect platform for carrying out this position.

She perches herself on top of the chosen appliance with her legs raised at a 65 degree angle to her body. He stands with his torso perpendicular to the top of the appliance and his hands positioned on both her legs and her back.

Best Practice: For higher intensity use an appliance with a strong vibration, such as a washing machine on a full spin cycle.

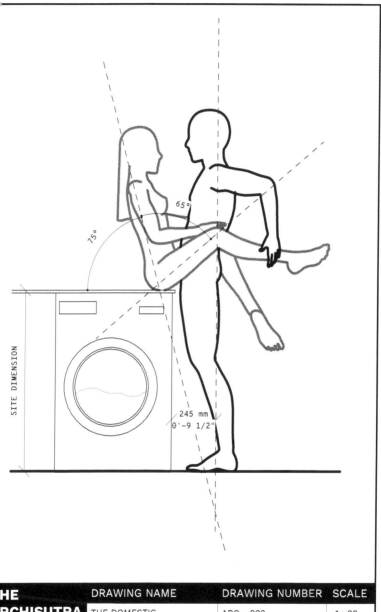

SITE DIMENSION

75°

65°

245 mm
0'-9 1/2"

THE ARCHISUTRA	DRAWING NAME	DRAWING NUMBER	SCALE
	THE DOMESTIC	ARC - 023	1 : 20

67

THE IKEA SALE

Typical Location: Residential
Sustainability: Medium

A tribute to the world's largest furniture retailer - IKEA, this position has been designed to be practiced on a pair of chairs, tables or any other flat-pack furniture. The dimensions of all IKEA products are available from their website and should be considered before commencing.

To initiate this position, he kneels on one IKEA product and faces the other. She fixes her head firmly on the second object while raising her legs on to his thighs. A strong core is required to bridge the distance between the furniture, so it is advisable to practice this position on the floor first.

Best Practice: Start by assembling the two pieces of furniture in close proximity. With practice, they can be moved further apart to increase the distance spanned by the position.

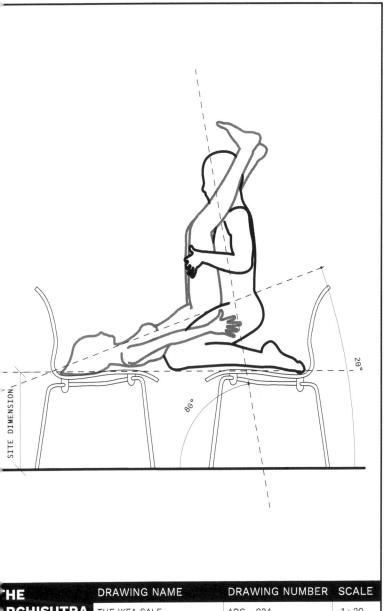

SITE DIMENSION

80°

20°

THE POMPIDOU

Typical Location: Residential

Sustainability: Medium

Taking inspiration from the Centre Pompidou in Paris, this position mimics the form of the building's iconic staircase, one of it's most striking features.

To start, he lies with his back on the floor and his head raised. She lowers herself on to him, kneeling with her head at a 30 degree angle to his feet and her hands fixed to the ground at either side of his legs.

Best Practice: This position is best practiced on a smooth surface to avoid risk of injury.

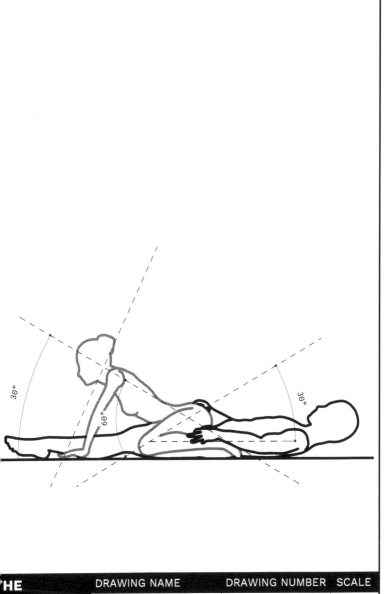

30°

60°

30°

THE
ARCHISUTRA

DRAWING NAME	DRAWING NUMBER	SCALE
THE POMPIDOU	ARC - 025	1 : 20

THE PETRONAS

Typical Location: Mixed-use

Sustainability: Low

The Petronas Towers in Malaysia, are an impressive pair of skyscrapers linked by a small bridge on the 41st and the 42nd floors. This position replicates its form as both bodies connect.

To perform *The Petronas*, both parties begin by standing opposite each other. She starts by lifting one of her legs over his shoulder, using it to pull him towards her. The position requires a high level of flexibility.

Best Practice: If you are attempting this position for the first time she should try to wrap her leg around his waist.

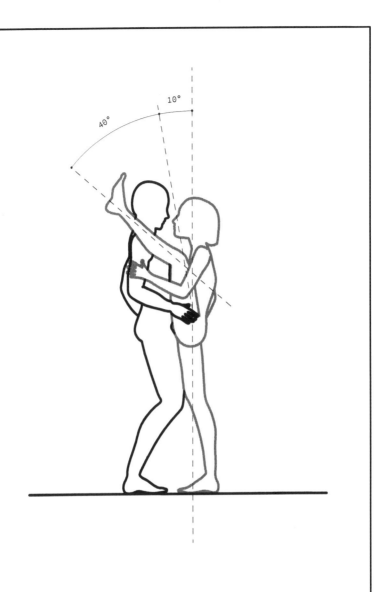

10°

40°

THE	DRAWING NAME	DRAWING NUMBER	SCALE
ARCHISUTRA	THE PETRONAS	ARC - 026	1 : 20

THE BRUTALIST

Typical Location: Mixed-use
Sustainability: Medium

The Brutalist style, popularised between 1950 and the 1970s is characterised by the use of large concrete forms with a raw appearance. *The Brutalist* position aims to follow some of the characteristics of the style.

This position is designed to be carried out on a concrete wall and floor. To begin, he manoeuvres his legs so that they are perpendicular to his body, which is touching both the wall and the floor. She then squats over him and faces the wall, holding his legs with her hands.

Best Practice: A rough wall should be reserved for the more experienced, to begin with find a smooth concrete wall.

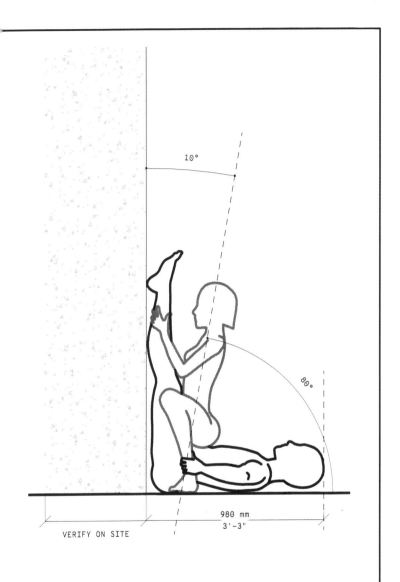

10°

80°

980 mm
3'-3"

VERIFY ON SITE

HUMAN FORMWORK

Typical Location: Residential

Sustainability: Medium

Named after the temporary moulds into which concrete or other similar materials are poured, *Human Formwork* uses his body to dictate her position.

He begins by lying or sitting down, before she lays on top facing him. He then adopts his chosen position, manipulating her form as he does. By angling his torso at 55 degrees he can take hold of her arms and pull her body closer.

Best Practice: This position is best performed on a low-friction surface, as her weight will make it hard for him to adjust his position.

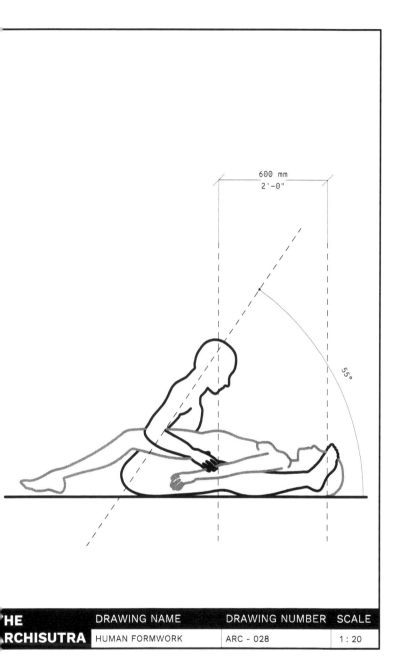

600 mm
2'-0"

55°

| THE | DRAWING NAME | DRAWING NUMBER | SCALE |
| **RCHISUTRA** | HUMAN FORMWORK | ARC - 028 | 1 : 20 |

THE BOTTOMAN

Typical Location: Residential
Sustainability: Medium

An often overlooked piece of furniture, the ottoman can be put to great use. It originated from the Ottoman Empire and was brought to Europe in the late 18th century.

To begin, she lies on her back on top of the ottoman with her head hanging over the edge. He kneels on the opposite side holding her lower thighs. He then lifts her legs to rest on his chest. Ottomans are usually padded to giving an extra bounce when performing this position.

Best Practice: If your ottoman has a storage section, it should be filled with books or other heavy objects to prevent it from sliding.

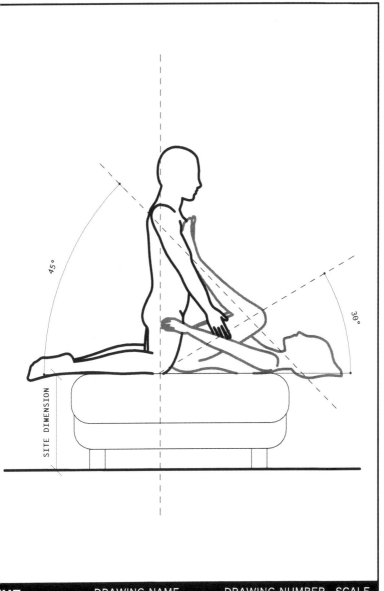

45°

30°

SITE DIMENSION

THE BACK SEAT DESIGNER

Typical Location: Residential
Sustainability: High

Named after co-workers who peer over your shoulder, stare at your screen while you are trying to work or give you unwelcome suggestions, these are the back seat designers.

In this position, he sits on an armchair of choice with his back straight. She sits on his lap and leans forward until her palms touch the floor. She then uses her knees and arms to move herself up and down.

Best Practice: Depending on the size of your armchair, it works best if he perches on the front end of the chair so that he can ensure a firm grip.

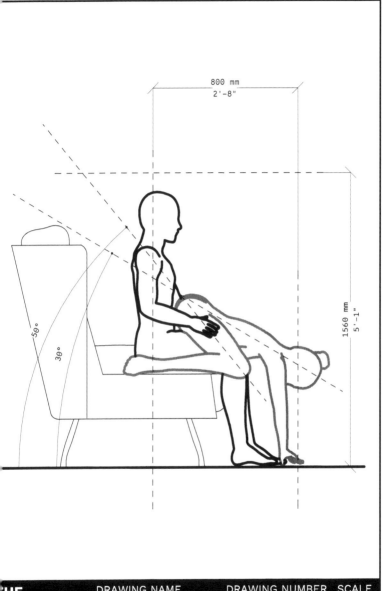

800 mm
2'-8"

1560 mm
5'-1"

50°

30°

THE ARCHISUTRA	DRAWING NAME	DRAWING NUMBER	SCALE
	THE BACK SEAT DESIGNER	ARC - 030	1 : 20

THE CLASSICAL

Typical Location: Mixed-use
Sustainability: High

The Classical is voted the world's favourite year on year, it's one that everyone knows, but the correct angles and dimensions will help you perfect it.

In this position, she kneels on all fours with her back parallel to the ground. He then positions himself behind her, with his body bent forward 15 degrees and his hands holding her hips.

Best Practice: Although this position is a classic, it can be performed in any location for a more unconventional twist.

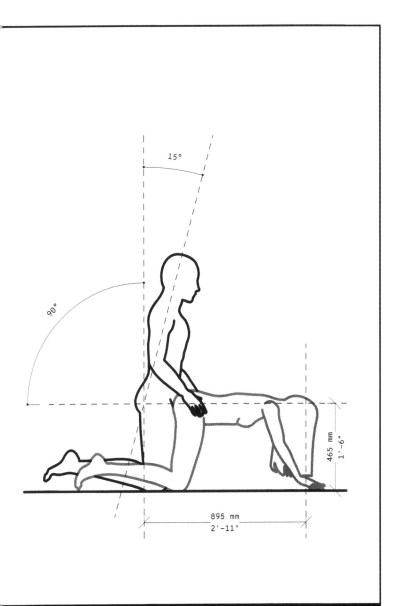

	DRAWING NAME	DRAWING NUMBER	SCALE
THE ARCHISUTRA	THE CLASSICAL	ARC - 031	1 : 20

THE NEO CLASSICAL

Typical Location: Mixed-use

Sustainability: Medium

The Neo Classical is a simple modern reinvention of the previous position, revived just as Neoclassical Architecture has been throughout history. Design revivals can sometimes be perceived as controversial, however this straightforward position is sure to be around for some time.

This position takes a similar form to *The Classical*, however he stands upright with a slight bend in his knee. She is on her feet, with her body bent at a 30 degree angle and her hands flat on the floor. This variation allows for a larger range of movement.

Best Practice: She should bend her knees slightly and use the edge of the bed as an extra support.

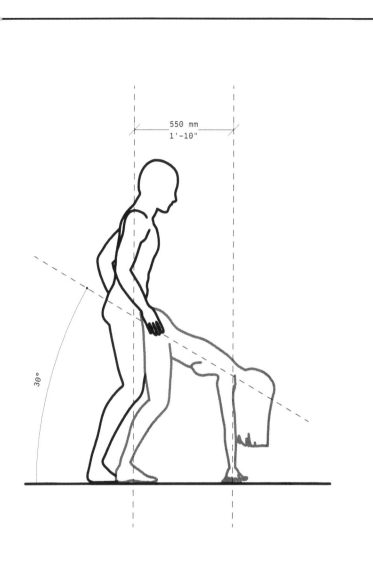

550 mm
1'-10"

30°

THE ARCHISUTRA	DRAWING NAME	DRAWING NUMBER	SCALE
	THE NEO CLASSICAL	ARC - 032	1 : 20

THE CANTILEVER

Typical Location: Mixed-use
Sustainability: Low

A structural cantilever is used in construction to support an overhanging element. This position draws upon this technique allowing movement to occur from only one pivotal point.

To get into this position, she bends forward with her head lifted off the floor and her arms reaching backwards. She grabs hold of his arms as he takes hold of her, ensuring a strong grip from both. She should be cantilevered over the floor by holding on to his arms.

Best Practice: Try getting into this position one arm at a time, trying to swing both arms around at the same time could cause injury.

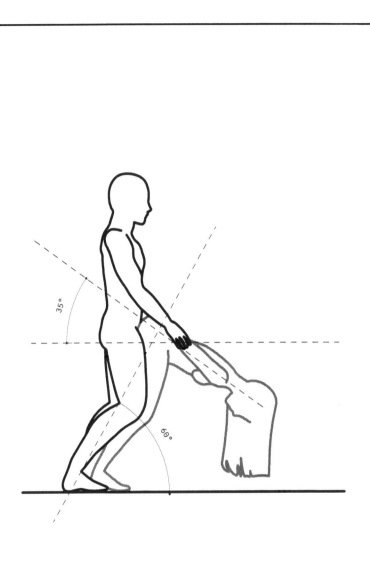

35°

60°

THE RCHISUTRA	DRAWING NAME	DRAWING NUMBER	SCALE
	THE CANTILEVER	ARC - 033	1 : 20

EXTERNAL WORKS

Typical Location: Mixed-use

Sustainability: High

Refer to drawing **031**.

Best Practice: *The Classical* can be reimagined in any external location. If privacy is a concern, the position should be practiced on an uninhabited or overgrown site.

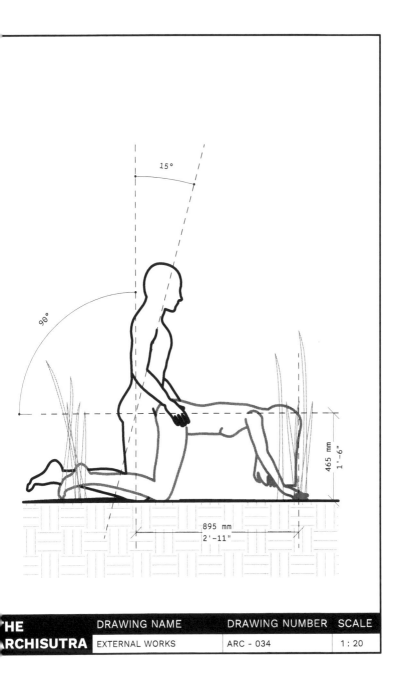

15°

90°

465 mm
1'-6"

895 mm
2'-11"

DRAWING NAME	DRAWING NUMBER	SCALE
EXTERNAL WORKS	ARC - 034	1 : 20

OSCAR'S

Typical Location: Residential
Sustainability: High

This position is a tribute to Oscar Niemeyer, a Brazilian architect and a true admirer of the female form.

In this position, he sits on the floor with his arms on the ground behind him and his body leaning back at 50 degrees. She sits directly above him, pressing her form into his chest and holding onto his thighs.

Best Practice: His body should provide a platform for her to lie on and support her weight entirely.

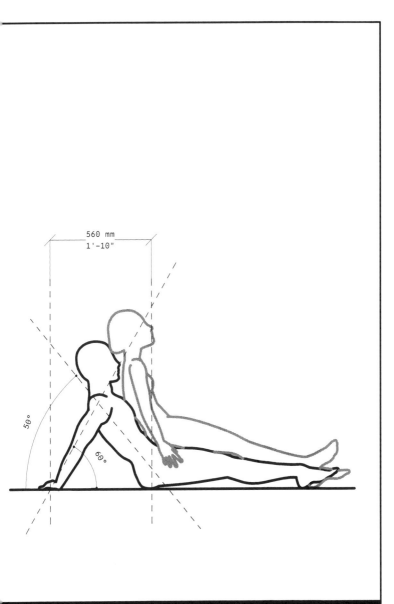

560 mm
1'-10"

50°

60°

THE ARCHISUTRA	DRAWING NAME	DRAWING NUMBER	SCALE
	OSCAR'S	ARC - 035	1 : 20

91

GET AN EIFFEL

Typical Location: Residential

Sustainability: Low

Inspired by the Eiffel Tower, constructed by Gustave Eiffel in 1889, *Get An Eiffel* recreates the iconic form of the tower using the human body.

To achieve this position, she begins by performing a handstand. He takes hold of her ankles to stop her falling as she lowers her abdomen onto his knees. He bends his knees slightly and holds onto her calves to give her a platform, as she grips her legs tightly around his thighs for stability.

Best Practice: If you find doing handstands difficult try practicing next to a wall for additional support.

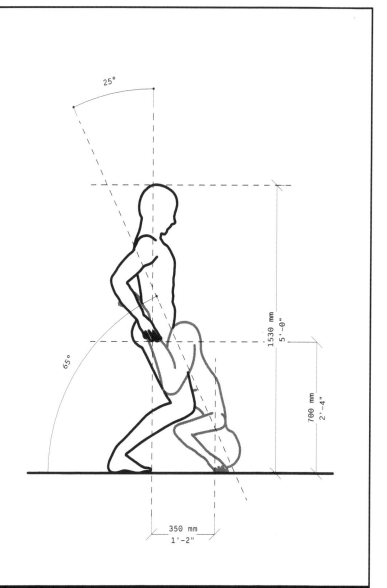

25°

65°

1530 mm
5'-0"

700 mm
2'-4"

350 mm
1'-2"

THE ARCHISUTRA	DRAWING NAME	DRAWING NUMBER	SCALE
	GET AN EIFFEL	ARC - 036	1 : 20

93

EAMES IT IN

Typical Location: Commercial

Sustainability: Low

Based around the iconic Aluminium chair designed by Charles and Ray Eames in 1958, *Eames It In* is the perfect position for an office environment. In 1969, a 'soft pad' version of the chair was released for increased comfort.

To *Eames It In*, the centre of the chair is placed approximately 725mm or 2'-4 ½" away from his starting position. She begins by standing between him and the chair and bends forwards to place her head on the seat. He then takes hold of one of her ankles, lifting her leg into the air.

Best Practice: These chairs come with or without wheels. To prevent injury, first attempt this position using the static version and only when you have more experience you should use the wheels.

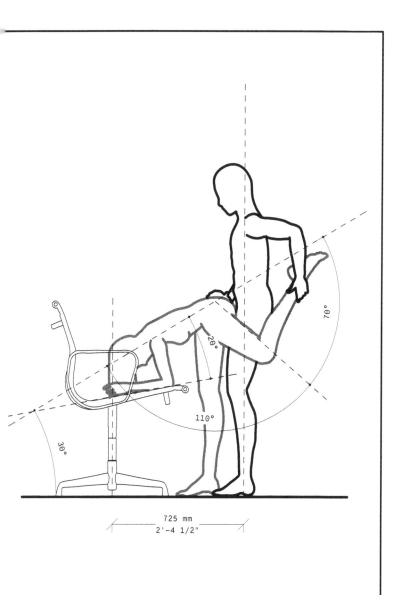

725 mm
2'-4 1/2"

20°

110°

70°

30°

DRAWING NAME	DRAWING NUMBER	SCALE
EAMES IT IN	ARC - 037	1 : 20

THE VERY GEHRY

Typical Location: Mixed-use

Sustainability: Low

Named after architect Frank Gehry, this position replicates the unusual forms and structures found within his designs.

To get into this position, she lies flat on the ground, lifts her lower body into the air and moves her knees towards her head. Once she is in this position, he squats on top of the platform she creates and leans forward 35 degrees to form a striking shape.

Best Practice: This position might seem quite advanced, but can be performed relatively easily.

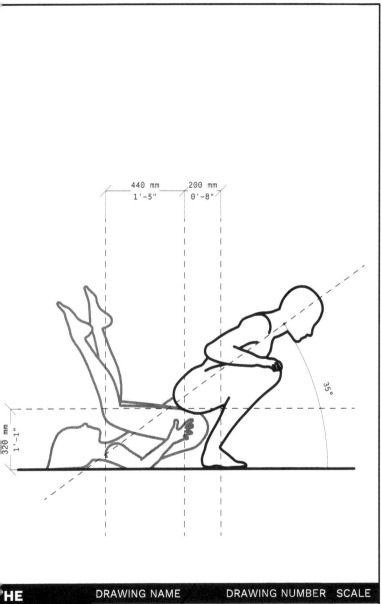

440 mm
1'-5"

200 mm
0'-8"

35°

320 mm
1'-1"

	DRAWING NAME	DRAWING NUMBER	SCALE
THE ARCHISUTRA	THE VERY GEHRY	ARC - 038	1 : 20

THE REAL FLEMISH BOND

Typical Location: Mixed-use
Sustainability: Medium

Typically bricks are laid using one of the following patterns: English bond, Flemish bond, Stretcher bond, Header bond or the Garden wall bond. *The Real Flemish Bond* is a position inspired by the most common type of brick bond, used universally to give a precise finish.

To begin, she lies on her front, lifting her torso slightly off the floor with her arms. He then lowers himself into a seated squat, keeping his back straight and his legs at a 45 degree angle to the ground.

Best Practice: The Real English Bond was deemed too explicit for publication.

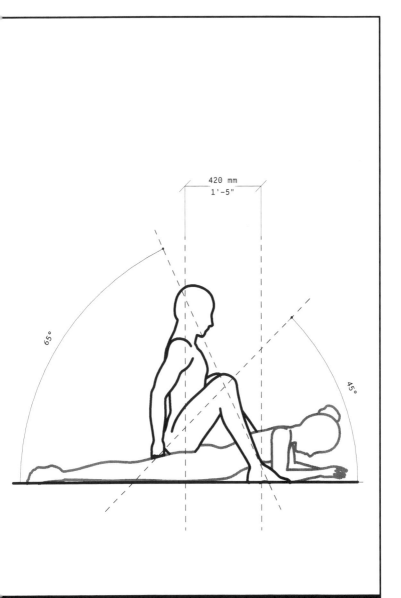

420 mm
1'-5"

65°

45°

THE	DRAWING NAME	DRAWING NUMBER	SCALE
ARCHISUTRA	THE REAL FLEMISH BOND	ARC - 039	1 : 20

THE POSTMODERN

Typical Location: Residential
Sustainability: Medium

Postmodernism emerged in the 1960s as a reaction against the lack of variety in modern architecture. Like postmodern architecture, this position offers complex forms, curves and asymmetry.

In this position, she forms a bridge at a 10 degree angle to the ground with a slight curve to her body. He gets into the kneeling position shown and holds on to her hips.

Best Practice: To lessen the strain on her arms, the edge of a sofa or bed could be used as a replacement for the bridge.

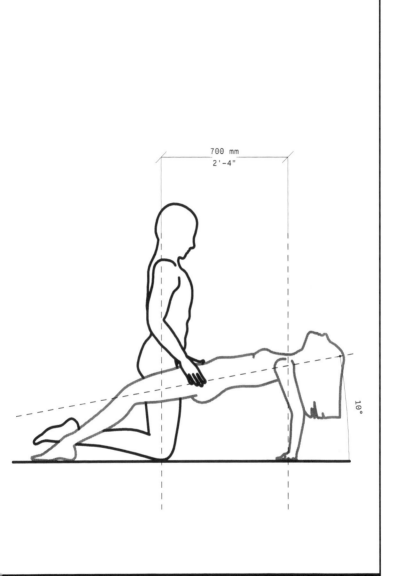

700 mm
2'-4"

10°

	DRAWING NAME	DRAWING NUMBER	SCALE
THE ARCHISUTRA	THE POSTMODERN	ARC - 040	1 : 20

PRAIRIE STYLE

Typical Location: Residential
Sustainability: High

Prairie Style, also known as the Prairie House Style, was popular in the late 19th and early 20th centuries in Midwestern America. The style was characterised by strong horizontal lines evoking the native prairie landscape.

In this position, he first sits down with his upper body perpendicular to the floor and his back at a sharp 90 degree angle. She stands over him before lowering her body to the ground with her head falling between his feet.

Best Practice: She should try and hover off the ground by lifting feet off the floor and resting her elbows on his legs.

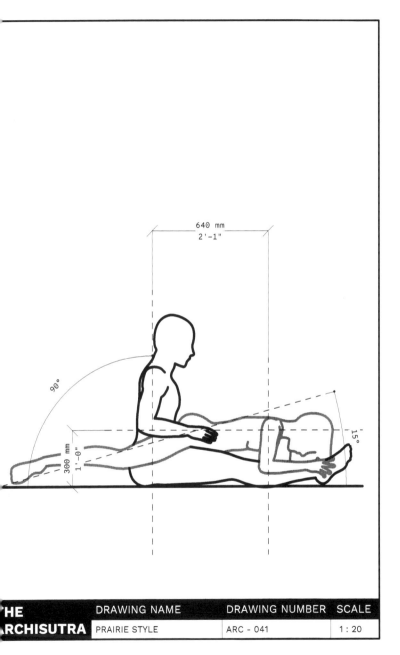

640 mm
2'-1"

90°

300 mm
1'-0"

15°

THE ARCHISUTRA	DRAWING NAME	DRAWING NUMBER	SCALE
	PRAIRIE STYLE	ARC - 041	1 : 20

THE LAP JOINT

Typical Location: Residential
Sustainability: High

A lap joint is used in carpentry to join materials by overlapping members. Inspired by this, *The Lap Joint* position creates a strong connection between both participants.

In this position, she begins lying flat on the floor with a pillow supporting her upper back. He lifts her legs above his pelvis at approximately 15 degrees and kneels between them.

Best Practice: Try experimenting with different sized pillows to find the angle that works best for you.

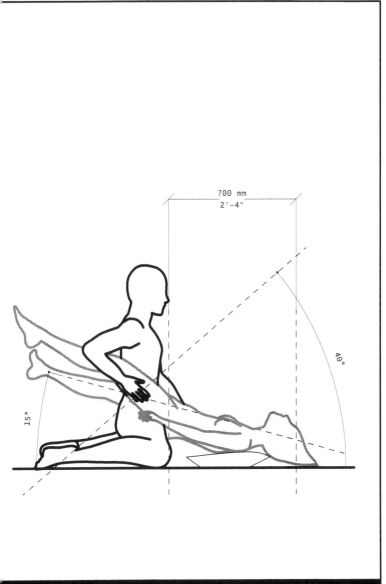

700 mm
2'-4"

40°

15°

THE ARCHISUTRA	DRAWING NAME	DRAWING NUMBER	SCALE
	THE LAP JOINT	ARC - 042	1 : 20

IN VITRA VERITAS

Typical Location: Mixed-use

Sustainability: High

Named after the Swiss furniture company, this position uses a Vitra chair, but can also be performed on any similar chair.

In this position, he sits on a chair with his back pressing firmly on the backrest. She sits facing him on his lap, leaning slightly backwards. By wrapping his arms around her body she can maintain the position for longer.

Best Practice: If you don't have the luxury of owning a Vitra chair, try to find a suitable alternative. For best results use a chair with some flexibility.

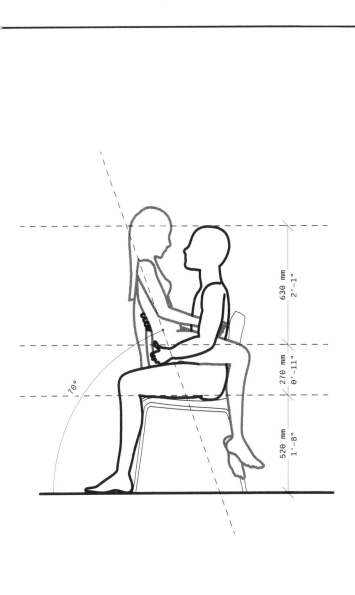

630 mm
2'-1"

270 mm
0'-11"

520 mm
1'-8"

70°

DRAWING NAME	DRAWING NUMBER	SCALE
IN VITRA VERITAS	ARC - 043	1 : 20

THE GAUDI

Typical Location: Mixed-use

Sustainability: Medium

Known for his very distinctive style, Spanish architect Antonio Gaudi was most recognised as a practitioner of Catalan Modernism. This position breaks away from normal arrangement and form, something Gaudi is famous for.

To perform this position he lies flat on the floor as she lowers herself on to him. Both participants begin facing forwards and once in position she rotates her body 90 degrees.

Best Practice: She should move in a circular motion, adjusting her movements in a rotational fashion.

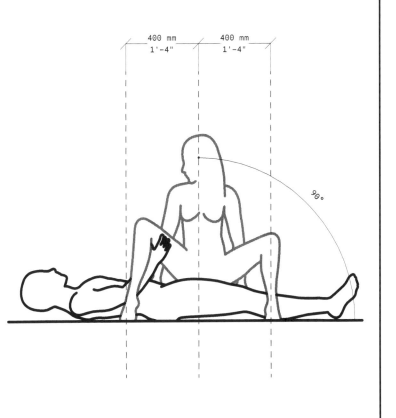

| 400 mm | 400 mm |
| 1'-4" | 1'-4" |

90°

THE	DRAWING NAME	DRAWING NUMBER	SCALE
ARCHISUTRA	THE GAUDI	ARC - 044	1 : 20

ROHE THE BOAT

Typical Location: Mixed-use
Sustainability: Medium

Named after German architect, Ludwig Mies van der Rohe, this position resembles a rower and is performed using similar actions.

In this position, he lies on the floor with his legs slightly spread. She sits on top with her body leaning forward at 40 degrees and her feet positioned inside of his legs. She can control the motion using both her legs and her arms, with her hands resting on his thighs.

Best Practice: She should move her hands back and forth down his legs in a similar movement to that of a rower.

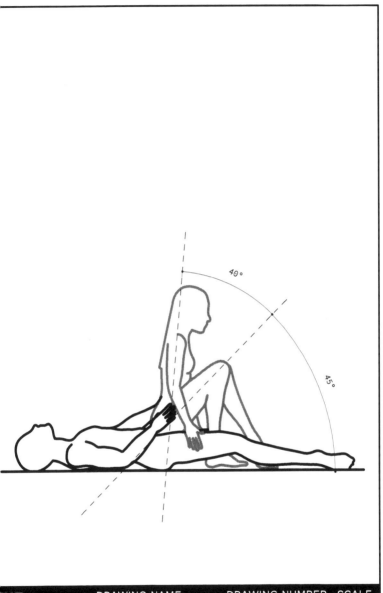

40°

45°

THE ENGINEER

Typical Location: Mixed-use
Sustainability: Low

Structural and Civil Engineers are needed calculate the stability, durability and rigidity of a construction. This position requires precise alignment and collaboration.

For this position, both participants adopt a squatting position. He gets into the squat first and once he is set up, she follows suit and positions herself in front of him and on to his lap.

Best Practice: This position is best performed on a soft or bouncy surface, allowing you to maintain the squat position for longer.

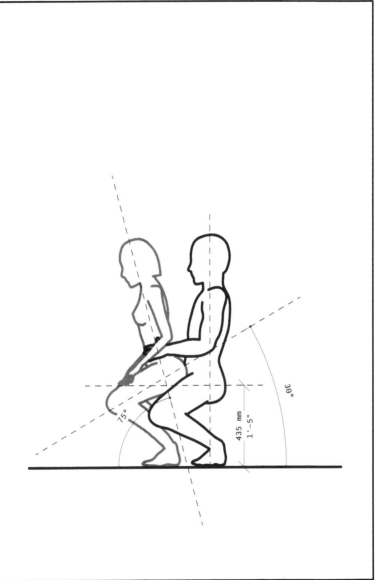

75°

30°

435 mm
1'-5"

113

THE ALL NIGHTER

Typical Location: Commercial
Sustainability: Medium

Usually taking place the evening before a deadline, an all nighter is an intensive period of work that continues throughout the night.

This position is performed while at your desk. She starts lying face down on the desk, keeping her feet on the ground at first. He stands behind her at the edge of the desk and lifts up her legs, keeping them bent upwards at a 45 degree angle.

Best Practice: Remember that you might have to work here in the future.

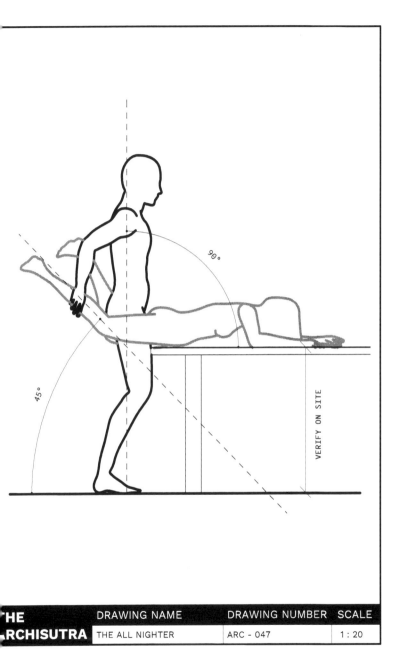

90°

45°

VERIFY ON SITE

YOU-VALUE

Typical Location: Residential

Sustainability: Medium

U-Values measure the insulative properties of a material, used in construction to test the environmental performance of buildings.

In this position, he sits on the ground with his legs crossed as she sits on his lap and wraps her legs around his back. She then works her legs up his body until they are positioned at at 40 degree angle to her body and can be rested on his shoulders. She can hold onto his knees for support.

Best Practice: If she starts to fall backwards she should hold onto his shoulders, he can hold her in place using his arms.

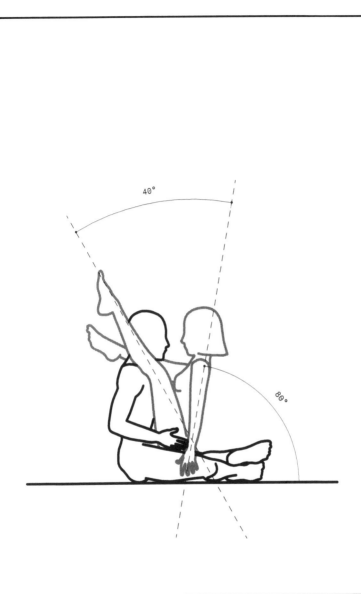

40°

80°

DRAWING NAME	DRAWING NUMBER	SCALE
YOU-VALUE	ARC - 048	1 : 20

THE TRELLICK

Typical Location: Residential
Sustainability: Medium

The Trellick Tower was designed by architect Erno Goldfinger and was completed in 1972. Its main feature is its lift and service tower that connects to the main building using access corridors. This advanced position mimics the structure of the tower and should be performed with caution.

To get into this position, both participants begin by standing upright, facing in the same direction. She bends forwards to form a handstand position and fully leans backwards on to him without extending her legs. Throughout the duration of the position, he supports her by holding on to her thighs.

Best Practice: He should bend his knees to help maintain stability, he should also hold on to her to prevent her from falling backwards.

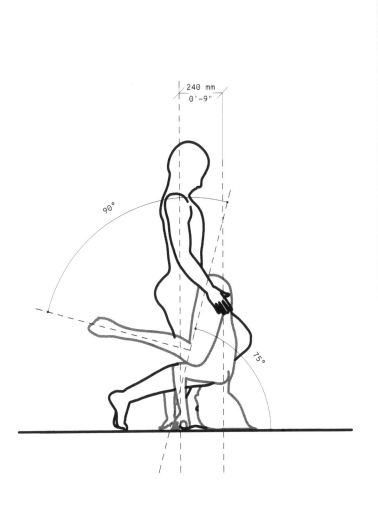

240 mm
0'-9"

90°

75°

THE GOLDEN RATIO

Typical Location: Mixed-use

Sustainability: Medium

The Golden Ratio is named and arranged after the mathematical ratio, which shows proportions which are believed to be aesthetically pleasing. Many twentieth-century architects have used this theory within their work.

For this position, she starts lying on the ground with her legs either side of him in a kneeling position. She then wraps her legs around his waist elevating her body as she pulls herself towards him. Her forearms should be flat on the ground to support her.

Best Practice: A pillow can be added to help support her and maintain the golden ratio.

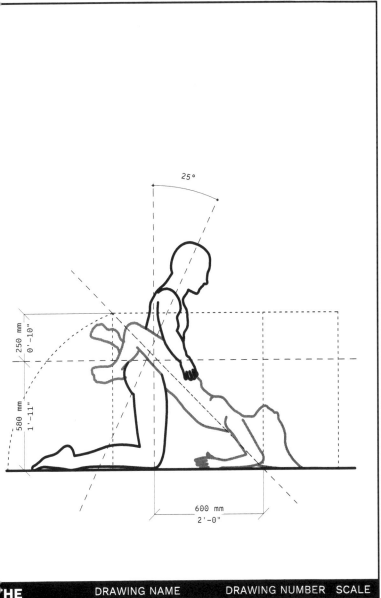

25°

250 mm
0'-10"

580 mm
1'-11"

600 mm
2'-0"

Made in the USA
San Bernardino, CA
07 July 2018